THE AUTHORITY GUIDE TO
MINDFUL LEADERSHIP

Simple techniques and exercises to manage
yourself, manage others and effect change

PALMA MICHEL

The Authority Guide to Mindful Leadership

Simple techniques and exercises to manage yourself, manage others and effect change

© Palma Michel

ISBN 978-1-909116-88-7
eISBN 978-1-909116-89-4

Published in 2017 by Authority Guides
authorityguides.co.uk

A CIP record of this book is available from the British Library.

Printed in the United Kingdom.

Contents

Part I My journey with meditation   1

    1. Changing times require new leadership skills   5

    2. Mindful leadership   13

Part II Managing yourself   19

    3. The starting point: hacking your nervous system   21

    4. Self-awareness as the first step to self-mastery   27

    5. Attention is a sought-after quality   35

    6. Leaders are not paid to be busy   41

    7. Leadership presence as a key leadership skill   45

Part III Managing others   51

    8. Authenticity builds trust and rapport   55

    9. Mastering communication   59

    10. Getting the most out of your team   71

    11. Building a culture for innovation   79

Contents

Part IV Effecting broader change   87

    12. Sustainability – acting today for tomorrow   91

About the author   95

Bibliography   97

Part I
My journey with meditation

I first got connected with meditation at the end of a yoga class in 1994. Like most people, I fell asleep during the meditation, as I was just so exhausted from attending law school during the day and working part-time in a blue-chip, strategy consulting firm in the evenings. However, something resonated with me and from that moment I knew that I would go much deeper into meditation at some later stage in my life. That time came when I moved to Hong Kong in 2006 and started practising yoga and meditation on a daily basis. The first time I noticed that I behaved somewhat differently from my colleagues was after the financial crisis. I had just been promoted to junior partner in a global executive search firm and had my first revenue responsibility. The external environment was uncertain, very volatile and there was pressure to bring in revenue for the firm, while at the same time our company was going through redundancy rounds. Clients were hesitant in making new hires and even if they had verbally agreed to sign a contract it often took weeks, if not months, for them to receive the internal approval. During this time I noticed that I remained very calm despite juggling a hectic, global 24/7 schedule with financial pressure and lots of uncertainty. I was able to put my head down and focus on the work that had to be done instead of worrying about the future or getting worked up about contracts that did not materialise. I was able to maintain equanimity and balance. One morning after a meditation class, in which I had experimented with courage and trust, I was sitting in my office, overlooking Pacific Place in Hong Kong, when I had a light-bulb moment. It was crystal clear to me that the experiential learning when I was sitting in meditation was closing the gap between intellectually knowing something and wanting to change and actually experiencing it in my body and mind and transforming my way of being. I was inspired to create a business that combines coaching and meditative wisdom and techniques to empower CEOs, founders, emerging leaders and high-potentials to access their full potential even, or particularly when, under pressure. I subsequently did all the necessary tuition including a two-year yoga and meditation teacher training (while I was still working as a headhunter), a teacher training in mindfulness-based stress reduction, courses in positive psychology and neuroscience and a professional training as a coach. Over the past three years I have introduced mindfulness to start-ups, global multinationals, small and medium-sized enterprises (SMEs) and creative businesses. In addition, I have used mindfulness and meditation to help c-suite individuals and start-up founders to access more of their leadership potential and creative genius.

On a personal level, the practice has given me more than I could have ever bargained for. While I was always quite a happy and optimistic person, there used to be a small background anxiety of something missing, of not being enough. It is through the dedicated practise of meditation and the methods from positive psychology that today the background anxiety has gone and has been replaced by a sense of fundamental wholeness, an inner peace that is always there in the foreground or at least the background, no matter what happens.

During over a decade as a board-level headhunter for two of the top five executive search firms, I have observed many examples of great leaders and many examples of not so great leaders and the damaging effects they can have on their teams and organisations. This led me on a quest to study how our brain works and what it is that can trip us up. I have observed the power of mindset and also observed what happens when leaders with great values seemingly act 'out of character' when under pressure. Having seen the transformative power of mindfulness practice in my own life, my coachees and in the organisations I work with, I am very excited about being able to share these practices now with a much broader audience through this book.

How to use this book

The book is split into four parts. There is this introduction, then managing yourself, followed by managing others and, finally, effecting broader change. Within Parts II to IV, each chapter contains guided reflections and exercises. You will gain the most value out of this book if you incorporate these exercises into your life and make them your own. It might be helpful to read one chapter and then pause to try out the exercises in your everyday life, before heading on to the next chapter. I will be sharing a lot of things with you in this book. Some of it will resonate with you and some maybe not so much. I encourage you to have an open mind, which is the first thing we practise in mindfulness, and to focus on the exercises that resonate with you and try them out for yourself. Ultimately it is one thing if they work for me or my clients and another one if they work for you. Some readers may find it helpful to write their thoughts down; for others that may be less helpful. Only you can judge what works for you.

Tell me and I forget, teach me and I may remember, involve me and I learn.

Benjamin Franklin

1. Changing times require new leadership skills

We are living in pressure cooker times and the digital age can be overwhelming to us: individually and collectively. There is a growing recognition of challenges presented by the pace of change, uncertainty, complexity and turbulence of doing business in the 21st century.

My work as board-level headhunter and executive coach has allowed me to travel to many different countries and meet leaders from different cultures and various walks of life. Yet, when discussing with CEOs, entrepreneurs, start-up founders and other senior decision makers, there is one common denominator describing the current business environment: the new normal is that nothing is normal and the only thing that is certain is that nothing is certain.

When working with senior executives, I usually use the term VUCA to describe the world we are operating in. VUCA was originally coined as a term by the US Army War College after the end of the Cold War, but is nowadays used as an accepted term in leadership circles to describe the world leaders operate in: VUCA stands for volatility, uncertainty, complexity and ambiguity.

It sounds like a cliché but we have experienced more change and volatility in the past eight years than in the past 30 years. Considering the latest advancements in technological innovation, the speed of change is not likely to slow down – if anything, it might accelerate even more drastically.

Most of my clients mention change as one of the key descriptors of the current business landscape. While a lot of uncertainty and change is related to the macro environment, the biggest change since the Industrial Revolution and the enormous speed undoubtedly comes from the pace of technological developments. This started with the invention of personal computers 30 years ago, and digital technology and smartphones have turned our private and working lives upside down. Today everyone carries a smartphone in their pocket, which is more powerful than our personal computers were just a few years ago, making knowledge readily available at our fingertips. Our children are learning coding in school, which is an entire new language and consequently a new way of seeing and understanding the world. In addition, artificial intelligence will soon replace some of our technical skills and roles. As a result, creativity and innovation are more than ever becoming distinguishing factors for success. In short, digital technologies have changed the world in ways that no one could have possibly predicted just a few years back.

Our modern work-life environment is dominated by information overload, 24/7 connectivity, continual interruptions and distractions through incoming email and various social media. This has made it increasingly difficult for leaders to focus and carve time out in their diaries to think and work strategically. Consequently, many leaders find themselves doing 'busy work' and reacting to what is urgent instead of strategic.

Today's world is complex and more interconnected and interdependent than ever before. The rise of the sharing economy, the 'Uberfication' of services and the shift of the power balance from companies to consumers have disrupted entire industries such as hospitality, mobility and financial services and put traditional business models under pressure. Future change will be dramatic on an economic and societal level. As a result, established businesses are required to take a critical look at their current business models. In order to thrive and not just merely survive, leaders and organisations need to fully embrace digitalisation and develop a more agile and entrepreneurial mindset and modus operandi. This means that leaders in the digital age are required to step out of their comfort zone and take bold risks.

Unlike leaders in traditional industries, start-up founders on the other hand are usually quite used to getting out of their comfort zone and to taking risks. Many follow the Silicon Valley motto, 'Move Fast and Break Things', and their entire business model is often built on venturing into something that has not been done before. The biggest challenges in start-ups are usually the pressure from investors, paired with the enormous volatility in growing a business, and often start-ups are faced with daily ups and downs, which can make it really hard to be decisive and take the right decisions amidst the emotional turmoil of building a business.

Even though the financial crisis happened over eight years ago, we are still dealing with some of its repercussions and today's world economic climate remains challenging and unpredictable. The Eurozone's struggle for stability including the uncertainty caused by Brexit, the European refugee crisis, the US elections and the slowing of the Chinese economy all impact the global economy.

Consequently, leaders are faced with uncertainty, and even outcomes from familiar actions are less predictable these days. The haziness of reality and the potential for misreading situations can cause confusion, often resulting in a freeze reaction for leaders. Today's challenges are new and different and, as such, require a different response.

In the workplace, this often translates into increased pressure on the individual. Leaders are required to do more with less in shorter time frames or to come up with creative ideas 'yesterday'. If they don't, they often feel that their head is on the line.

There is also a growing recognition among leaders that they can no longer leave the sole responsibility for global challenges that impact humankind to governments. The impact of climate change, deforestation and a potential water shortage require collaboration across different sectors, disciplines and geographies. The need to look at sustainability is partially driven by commercial considerations as leaders recognise that they might not have a supply chain if they don't tackle environmental issues. It is also partially driven by the change in consumer power, with consumers valuing sustainability, and partially by a new and more conscious brand of leaders. In addition, millennials are a different kind of 'breed' to manage. Having grown up with uncertainty, they are no longer looking for a secure lifetime career but often an inspiring workplace with a mission and a purpose that they can identify with.

In an environment where shareholders, customers and employees lose trust quickly, there is also increasing demand for strong corporate cultures based on purpose and a robust ethical compass.

Leaders recognise that new rules of engagement are needed

The old ways of operating no longer work and leaders need new rules of engagement to master current challenges. External forces mean that organisations and leadership teams need to change and adapt as quickly as possible. Leaders are often required to find solutions off the beaten track. Today's leadership challenges are complex and complex challenges require different leadership strategies. The change we are currently facing cannot be solved by just technical expertise but is adaptive in nature, which requires us to do something different. In today's VUCA world, leaders cannot just rely on what they think they know but have to be comfortable in the space of 'not knowing'. They have to remain open and be agile learners in every situation in order to stay connected, engaged and relevant to the people they are leading.

The problem is that whenever there is uncertainty or pressure, such as in the current business environment, there is a tendency to jump to conclusions, to react unconsciously, to procrastinate or to collapse the creative rollercoaster prematurely – in short, a tendency to get out of the unknown or uncertainty as quickly as possible, without being aware of the possible long-term consequences of the actions taken. What tends to trip us up is our very own nervous system: we evolved in circumstances that did not change as quickly and as drastically as the current environment. According to neuroscientist Rick Hanson (n.d.), our 'nervous system has been evolving for 600 million years, from ancient jellyfish to modern humans'. Back many tens of thousands of years ago, the brains of our hunter-gatherer ancestors were continuously screening the environment for danger and put them into a fight–flight–freeze reaction whenever they heard the slightest sound in the bushes. At the time this was very useful, as it could have been a tiger wanting to eat them for lunch. Even though we evolved as humans and are no longer living in the bush, our brains have unfortunately not evolved as much and we still have this ancient part of the brain, called the amygdala. Assuming that you are not managing a wildlife camp in Africa or are a commander in a war zone, it is unlikely that your life is actually in danger – even though it might feel that way when you are facing challenges at work.

However, your amygdala is still on the alert and will likely, in the case of dealing with uncertainty, the unknown or when you feel under pressure, hijack your executive brain (Goleman, 2006). The executive brain is responsible for focus, long-term thinking, strategic thinking, impulse control and positive outlook. In the 21st century, the cause of this hijack could be a look at your full inbox, a thought about the next board meeting, the budget meeting or being questioned by your chairman.

Once your amygdala is on, your body produces the stress hormone cortisol, your immune system, reproductive organs and digestive system shut down and your muscles tense up, which causes you to feel stressed and often act in ways that you later regret. The other problem is that functional magnetic resonance imaging (fMRI) scans show that what mostly switches on our amygdala are not even external circumstances but our very own thoughts about and appraisal of a situation. As such, a tendency to worry about the future, ruminate about the past or project a negative outcome of a meeting has direct implications on our leadership ability in the present moment. In addition, our brain also has a tendency for creating worst-case scenarios. Maybe the following situation sounds familiar to you: you are stuck in traffic and your thoughts are 'I am going to be late for a meeting, I am going to lose this client, I am going to lose my job.' From my experience, worst-case scenarios hardly ever happen, and even if they do, we tend to largely underestimate our ability to deal with them in the moment. Yet thoughts can put us into a negative downward spiral. Daniel Goleman, the 'father' of emotional intelligence (EQ), says a high IQ is not worth much if you are spending most of your days in the more primitive parts of your brain.

A leader's shadow is very long and wherever they put their attention, the organisation follows. When leaders are stuck in a reactive fight–flight–freeze cycle, this usually affects direct reports and cascades down through the organisation.

In order to initiate or guide skilful change, leaders need to be present to (or aware of) what is here, not what they thought would be here, could be here, should be here or to what was here yesterday. Leaders also need to be able to hold ambiguity and be comfortable with the unknown. They do not only need tools to manage the outer landscape and what is happening around them, but they also need tools to manage their inner landscape. In many ways, the 'inside job' determines the success of the 'outside job'.

Reflection on change

What is your relationship to change (do you embrace it, resist it or are you neutral towards it)?

Reflection on uncertainty

When faced with uncertainty, what is your habitual course of action?

I've lived through some terrible things in my life, some of which actually happened.

Mark Twain

2. Mindful leadership

In the past few years, mainly as a response to today's leadership challenges, a variety of management schools (including Harvard, Stanford, INSEAD, Stockholm School of Economics, LSE, Darden and NYU Stern School of Business) have introduced mindfulness/contemplative sciences into their MBA or leadership programmes. At the same time, companies including investment banks such as Goldman Sachs, Barclays, JP Morgan, global multinationals including General Mills, Apple and Google, FTSE 100 companies such as Transport for London and Unilever and consulting companies such as McKinsey and Ernst & Young have started introducing mindfulness programmes to their employees. In addition, members of the UK Parliament and the US Congress regularly get together for mindfulness sessions. In the UK, the Mindfulness All-Party Parliamentary Group has developed a report, 'Mindful Nation UK' (2015), which includes a section on mindfulness in the workplace.

However, despite the rise of mindfulness in management schools, the workplace and the government, it can only partially be explained by today's leadership challenges. The popularity of mindfulness has also been helped by advances in contemplative neuroscience, which indicate that mindfulness training has the power to alter our brain structure for the better. Professor Richard Davidson from the University of Wisconsin Madison, one of the leading neuroscientists researching the effects of mindfulness training on the brain, suggests that mindfulness training can change our in-built response to pressure, demands and uncertainty by strengthening our executive brain and by increasing the white matter between the amygdala and the executive brain. By dampening the amygdala, the executive brain is able to quieten down signals associated with negative emotions. As a result, we get triggered less often, and when we do, we gain the ability to step back, become aware of what is happening and, as such, can make a choice to respond differently this time (Begley and Davidson, 2012). Recent research (Zeidan et al., 2009; Congleton et al., 2015; Seppala, 2015; Reynolds, 2016) suggests that mindfulness training, among many other benefits, strengthens resilience and the ability to focus, supports decision-making and strategy, and increases authenticity and EQ as well as creates more compassionate leaders. Neuroscientist Britta Hölzel even goes as far as to say '[mindfulness is] a "must-have" [for executives]: a way to keep our brains healthy, to support self-regulation and effective decision-making capabilities, and to protect ourselves from toxic stress' (Congleton et al., 2015). Furthermore, the 2007 RESPONSE project, funded by the European Commission 6th Framework Programme, suggests that mindfulness-based leadership trainings were the most effective tool to lead to greater levels of corporate social responsibility (CSR), and to increased integrity and ethics (INSEAD, 2007).

What is mindful leadership?

Whenever I introduce mindfulness to leaders, I usually have to start by speaking about what mindfulness is not. Common misconceptions include thinking that mindfulness is the same as relaxation, just esoteric mumbo jumbo or a religious practice.

The UK All-Party parliamentary initiative defines mindfulness as:

> Paying attention to what's happening in the present moment in the mind, body and external environment, with an attitude of curiosity and kindness. It is typically cultivated by a range of simple meditation practices, which aim to bring a greater awareness of thinking, feeling and behaviour patterns, and to develop the capacity to manage these with greater skill and compassion.
>
> Mindfulness All-Party Parliamentary Group,
> 'Mindful Nation UK'

Mindfulness stands in direct contrast to habitual, unconscious 'autopilot' modes of mind and behaviour and is a quality of conscious awareness, which is characterised by clarity and the direct experiencing of actions, thoughts, sensations, emotions and behavioural patterns in the present moment.

Mindfulness is a secular contemplative practice, which has two elements: the formal element, which is called meditation, and the informal element, which applies what we learned during the formal practice to our leadership and lives at large.

Looking at the roots of the word meditation, meditation derives from the Latin *meditatio*, which comes from the verb *meditari*, meaning to think, to contemplate. The Tibetan word for meditation, *Gom*, which means to become familiar with, has the strong implication of training the mind to be familiar with states that are beneficial: concentration, compassion, correct understanding, patience, humility and perseverance (Wikipedia, n.d.).

In the formal meditation practice, we focus our attention on our breath, bodily sensations, thoughts, emotions or sensory perceptions. By training our attention in meditation, we create self-awareness. In addition, we hone skills such as courage, acceptance, patience, curiosity, equanimity, clarity, an attitude of non-judging, calmness and compassion.

Mindfulness is not just another practice that we add on to our already too busy lives, but an innate quality that we all already have and can rediscover through practice. Mindfulness does not require us to separate ourselves from our life, but invites us to engage with it in a different way. I often like to use the example of wine tasting, which exemplifies how an activity that many of us routinely do without thinking about it can be experienced in a very different way if we bring a heightened level of attention to it. When we go to a wine tasting, we engage all of our senses: we look at the bottle, we smell the cork, look at the colour of the wine in the glass, and we smell the wine and take a small sip to taste. The invitation is to bring a similar kind of awareness to our minds and behaviour in the present moment when we are meeting a client, during our team meeting, while negotiating a deal or on the golf course. We are invited to question the opinions, beliefs and assumptions that we are presented with and to stay flexible. By applying this quality of awareness to our minds, we are less prone to react from a habitual unconscious place but gain the freedom to base our actions on conscious intentions.

Mindfulness and leadership

When mindfulness is applied to leadership, there are three different components:

- How a leader manages themselves
- How a leader interacts with and manages others
- How a leader effects change in the broader system

So a mindful leader is not just a leader who meditates, but a leader who manages from the inside out and in the service of others. Mindfulness allows leaders to become more comfortable with the space of 'not knowing' and to manage their inner landscape and get into a different relationship with their distractions, thoughts, emotions and stress. It trains their ability to stay focused and create mental space, and increases their awareness of self, others and the broader system they operate in. This allows leaders to gain perspective and skilfully respond to what any given situation requires as well as to increase their resilience and learning agility. Increased awareness of others, especially when it comes from a compassionate place, allows leaders to become more effective relationship managers. Mindful leaders build mindful cultures, which are not purely driven by greed but are more cooperative in nature and take into account the company's role and responsibility in the broader system.

Reflection on mindfulness

We all have experienced moments of mindfulness and presence. Take a moment to reflect on a time when you were completely immersed in an activity or environment, totally in the flow or completely present in the moment. For some of us, that is when we are in nature, maybe watching a beautiful sunset, observing the waves on a beach or while skiing in the mountains. For others, it is when doing a hobby, being immersed in a creative activity or a stimulating discussion at work, or with a friend. Just notice whatever comes up for you.

Check-in exercise

You can do this exercise sitting on your office chair or you may want to find a more comfortable seat. Close your eyes for a moment or rest your gaze at a point in front of you. Then notice what is present (e.g. what you are aware of right now) at the level of your mind, the level of your body and the underlying feeling. This means noticing what thoughts you are having, what sensations you are experiencing in your body and what kind of feelings you can sense.

Part II: Managing yourself

Management guru Peter F. Drucker said, 'we cannot manage others unless we learn to manage ourselves first' (Drucker School of Management, 2016). Mindfulness helps us to develop the capacity to self-manage and self-regulate, to be able to manage ourselves to be in the optimum state to respond to whatever situation we are in – from dealing with staff, responding to a crisis situation, leading a business meeting, to being more relaxed and able to sleep at night or spending time with the family. It allows us to get more in touch with our intrinsic wholeness and inner wisdom, so that we learn how to listen to our full being and not just our minds. This allows us to lead from a place of centredness and calmness.

Being fully present is essential in the world of sports, a profession that has for decades used mindfulness meditation and other mind-training tools such as self-hypnosis.

Like athletes, leaders cannot win when they are mentally defeated. An athlete who 'doesn't have a clear head' is unlikely to perform in a manner that will prove successful. As such, both leaders and athletes need to develop effective tools that can help them in keeping a clear mind when under pressure. A number of the world's leading athletes and CEOs have been 'coming out' as meditators in recent years. They include Arianna Huffington, co-founder of *The Huffington Post*; Steve Jobs, the late Apple CEO; Rose Marcario, CEO Patagonia; Tiger Woods; Novak Djokovic; and Oprah Winfrey. As anyone who's ever played a sport knows, the biggest opponent is usually inside our own minds. Mindfulness gives you ways to come to terms with this inner opponent.

3. The starting point: hacking your nervous system

We tend to assume that we are conscious human beings that make conscious leadership decisions, but that is unfortunately not always the reality in our boardrooms and daily lives. According to Harvard Professor Ellen Langer, most of us are on autopilot virtually all of the time. As we saw in Chapter 2, the current environment has a tendency to trip up our nervous system when we are faced with change, pressure or uncertainty. Whenever our amygdala is triggered, we are reactive and the focus is on short-term, impulse and speedy decisions without being able to take long-term consequences into consideration.

Our autonomic nervous system consists of the sympathetic and the parasympathetic nervous system. The parasympathetic nervous system is also called our rest and digest response and marks a state of equilibrium. The sympathetic nervous system (fight–flight–freeze response) kicks in whenever the amygdala is sending a signal of distress. It basically prepares our body for a threat and is responsible for a variety of physical changes, including speeding up our heart rate and breathing, and releasing stress hormones such as cortisol into our bloodstream. At that moment we have no space in our minds and if there is no space, there is no choice and we have no options. We might think we are making a choice but we are actually not; the behaviour is automatic, habitual and reactive.

Asked about their values, the majority of leaders have good values and intentions – yet so many good and well-trained leaders fall short of their potential or lack integrity when the going gets tough and they feel their necks are on the line. It is not because they have 'bad characters' per se or consciously intended to harm their corporations, employees, peers or customers. They fall short because their amygdala is hijacking the executive brain, which makes us do things that are not very smart and which might have negative consequences for ourselves, the people we are leading and our company. In the worst case it also affects the community and industry we operate in, as seen during the financial crisis. Once the amygdala is in charge, our best intentions and values can get obscured and a 'me first' attitude prevails. The result is often a mismatch between what a leader preaches and his or her actual demonstrated behaviour. This tends to lead to a loss in trust and credibility. Once the trust is damaged, it is very hard to repair it.

For example, I worked with a CEO who had amazing values and was very passionate about building a culture of trust, innovation, empowerment and open discussion. Yet whenever he felt under pressure, he had a tendency to become closed, defensive and committed to being right. In those moments, he would shut people down. As he had a very impressive background and people looked up to him, this led to people feeling scared when they had to discuss their ideas with him. They often procrastinated and tried to hide the mistakes they made, and in many ways he created the exact opposite culture of what he had intended.

Another example is a chief financial officer (CFO) who finds herself getting aggressive and defensive whenever she gets questioned in a board meeting. While she intellectually understands that this is to be expected, there is a deep rooted belief that she is not respected because of her humble upbringing and a need to prove her worth, which trips her up in these situations.

A leader's behaviour determines to a large extent how the rest of the organisation behaves.

The starting point for you as a leader, before you do anything else, must be to learn how to 'hack' your nervous system in order to access your full leadership potential in all situations and remain calm and focused even under pressure or when faced with change and uncertainty. The two things that prevent us from being centred are negative thoughts and negative emotions. Hacking your nervous system creates space in your mind, which gives you conscious choices and allows you to respond rather than habitually react.

We can work with mindfulness of breath and bodily sensations to calm down our nervous system or remain more alert and present in any given situation. When we are stressed, the autonomic nervous system is out of balance. Our breath becomes short and shallow and we breathe from the chest. We can consciously activate the parasympathetic nervous system with a breathing exercise. When the parasympathetic nervous system kicks in, our breathing slows down, our heart rate and blood pressure drop and the body goes back to a state of calm. Whenever we find ourselves emotionally triggered, we can learn how to calm ourselves down by applying simple breathing techniques to kick into the parasympathetic nervous system and slow down.

In my experience and from what neuroscience tells us, taking our seat to meditate is one of the most effective ways of hacking our nervous system in the long run. We take care of our bodies every day by brushing our teeth and taking a shower, and some of us try to have a healthy diet. In a similar way, it is crucial for leaders to take care of their minds on a daily basis.

Breathing exercise to kick in the parasympathetic nervous system

This breathing exercise will help to calm down your nervous system. It can be done sitting, standing or lying down. You may want to use it when you feel triggered during a conversation, when you have difficulties falling asleep or seeing your full inbox.

Take a few, conscious breaths through your nostrils, inhaling deeply all the way into your abdomen and exhale through your mouth with pursed lips. Count to two on the inhale and elongate your exhale by counting to four. After a few breaths, count to three on the inhale and elongate your exhale counting to six. If you feel comfortable with this, count to four on the inhale and elongate your exhale to the count of eight.

Meditation exercise

Find a comfortable meditative posture, with your feet flat on the floor and a straight spine. Close your eyes or rest your gaze at a point in front of you. Start by taking three to six deep abdominal breaths by breathing in through your nostrils and filling up your abdomen as if it were a balloon. Slowly exhale through your mouth. Then allow your breath to be as it is and place one hand on your abdomen. Notice the subtle movement of the abdominal walls expanding and collapsing. Once you have familiarised yourself with this subtle movement, start to count your exhalations until you reach 30 counts. (A breathing meditation can be found on my website: palmamichel.com/breathing-meditation/)

Figure 1 A comfortable meditative posture

Tips on how to start your meditation practice

- Make a formal commitment with yourself to sit every day for meditation practice.

- You don't have to sit in a yogic posture; just sit on a chair with your feet flat on the floor.

- Observe your breath, by paying attention to its inflow and outflow. Count each exhalation.

- Don't try to empty your mind or stop your thoughts. Allow the thoughts to be; just come back to your breath over and over again.

- Like training for a marathon, start with a length of time that you can do every day (for example three minutes), which challenges you but does not feel like a chore.

- After a few weeks of practice, you will feel comfortable with your chosen time; slowly build up your practice by increasing the time every few weeks until you are doing at least 10–15 minutes per day.

- Regularity is key; in order to strengthen your attention muscle it is better to practise three minutes every day, rather than one hour each Sunday.

4. Self-awareness as the first step to self-mastery

Self-awareness is the first step to self-mastery and it really is at the heart of EQ. According to Daniel Goleman (2006), self-awareness means a deep understanding of your emotions, strengths, weaknesses and drives. A person who is very self-aware is neither overly critical nor unrealistically hopeful. They know what makes themselves tick, and are aware of their emotional triggers, thoughts, emotions, values, goals and habitual patterns. They are aware of their psychology and physiology and of why they react to things the way they do. Maybe they are even aware of their deep core beliefs that often operate below the level of consciousness and influence our attitudes and the way we respond to things. Self-awareness also includes being aware of the storylines that we have in our heads about who we are, what happened to us in the past and so on.

When we are sitting in the formal mindfulness practice, in meditation, we are entering a space of 'not knowing'. We are becoming aware of our thoughts, emotions and sensations in the present moment. We are becoming the witness: stepping back and watching thoughts and feelings that arise, not totally identifying with them.

There is generally no hiding when we face ourselves on the 'cushion'. As a rule of thumb, whatever shows up during meditation is a mirror-like reflection of what is present in our lives in general. So if we feel restless, impatient or bored during the meditation, it tends to show up in other parts of our lives and vice versa. When we sit, we get to know ourselves – including the parts that we would not necessarily like to share in a job interview or on a first date. But the more we can be with tension, anger, discomfort, boredom, impatience and embrace them instead of pushing them away, the more authentic we become. We also come to see that we are not a fixed, permanent entity, but rather an accumulation of thoughts, emotions and sensations, which are changing all the time. Once we realise that, changing unskilful behaviour and habits becomes a lot easier.

Mindfulness training increases a leader's self-awareness. Increased self-awareness increases a leader's choice to step out of unconscious habitual behaviours. According to research it is estimated that approximately 40 per cent of what people do on a daily basis is habitual and automatic, meaning that individuals do not make conscious choices about their behaviour. Through the course of the day, hundreds of habitual patterns and reactions are going on without you consciously noticing it. It takes awareness of what you are doing and conscious effort to change existing behaviour (Fox, 2012).

Having self-awareness gives us greater capacity to stand back and put things into perspective. It creates the reflective space where we can see everything that is happening, yet are not driven by it like a rudderless sailboat in the ocean. As a result we gain a choice-point and can possibly respond in a different way.

Awareness of being triggered

At any point, a leader is either triggered and in their stress zone or they are in their control zone. Increased self-awareness naturally leads to better self-management. Being aware of being triggered is the first step to changing your behaviour. Finding yourself triggered in any way (for example blaming others, being defensive or closed) is an indication that your amygdala is running the show. In those moments, you can use mindfulness of breath to calm down your nervous system and to move back into your control zone.

Reflection on being in the stress zone

What are the situations, people or environments where you find yourself triggered? How does it feel being in your stress zone? Does it have an effect on your ability to take productive action in the moment?

Exercise for getting back into your control zone

The next time you find yourself triggered, move your attention away from the thoughts in your head and bring your attention to your breath. Take at least five deep inhalations and exhalations. The trick here is to elongate your exhalation to calm down your nervous system and send your amygdala back to sleep. Count to four on the inhalation and to eight on the exhalation.

Awareness of the interplay of thoughts, emotions and sensations

Living in a human body, our moment-to-moment experience is composed of thoughts, emotions and physical sensations. Research with 'meditation champions' like senior Tibetan monks shows that every emotional reaction is an interplay between sensations in the body, thoughts and the emotional reaction. Usually an emotional reaction lasts up to 90 seconds. What can prolong this are our thoughts about the situation, which create additional sensations and feed the emotions (Bolte Taylor, 2008). In some ways it is like a self-perpetuating drama triangle.

It is useful to be aware of what usually happens in your body before or right at the moment when you become worried, angry, closed or defensive. After being asked to observe what happens, some of the things my clients report back is that they start pacing around, their breath becomes shallow, they might feel heat in their chest or wrinkle their forehead and notice that their muscles tense up. If we know these things about ourselves, then we can actively do something to calm down our nervous system by focusing on our breath or remove ourselves from the situation and ask for a break before we create damage to our reputation or the people we are leading.

Moving the attention away from the thoughts and the emotion and directing it to the sensations in the body can break this cycle as well. In these moments we can bring curiosity to the sensations in the body and use this to return to the present moment. We can also do the previous breathing exercise to get us back into the control zone.

Reflection on the interplay of thoughts, emotions and sensations

This exercise can be done with your eyes closed or open. Find a comfortable posture and try to notice what is present right now at the level of your thoughts, emotions and physical sensations. Then contemplate how they are relating to each other. You can expand this reflection and think about the last time that you felt angry: what were the thoughts, emotions and sensations in your body? The next time you feel angry, frustrated or stuck, bring the same kind of awareness to the situation.

Awareness of the quiet inner voice

Our innate wisdom often shows up as a quiet inner voice or a feeling in the body. It is a distinct knowing that something is right or wrong for us, yet every so often we ignore it. The inner voice of intuition is always silent to the outside. Unlike our loud voice, which comes with a variety of arguments of why we should or shouldn't do something, the inner voice of intuition never justifies itself. Mindfulness practice helps us to become more in tune with our intuition, so that we learn how to listen to our full being and not just our minds.

Reflection on intuition

How in tune do you currently feel with your intuition? Do you listen to your gut feelings? Take a moment to remember the last time you made a bad decision. Do you remember if you went with or against the quiet inner voice?

Awareness of being on autopilot

According to Langer (Ayala, 2014), 'most of us are on autopilot virtually almost all of the time'. Our minds might be stuck in thoughts about the past, replaying an earlier conversation in our mind, only this time we are saying something much smarter or more powerful. If our minds are not in the past, they tend to plan for or worry about the future. You might have previously experienced driving to work and upon arrival not really knowing 'who' had been driving the car, as you were not aware of driving. Or, like me, you might have tried opening your front door with your Oyster card or used your home key to get into the Tube. In addition, we have previously seen that a large portion of what we do all day is automatic and repetitive behaviour. We sleep on the same side of the bed, eat the same breakfast and take the same route to work every day. When we are on autopilot, not only are we not making conscious choices, we are also not connected with the people we are leading. We become 'human thinkings' rather than human beings and miss much of what happens in our environment and lives at large. The more we are aware of being on autopilot, the easier it is to change and become more present in our lives and to the people we are leading.

Reflection on being on autopilot

Just think for a moment how often do you find yourself being on autopilot. Then observe yourself over the next week and notice every time it happens.

Reflection on being present

The more you discover how to bring a clear and fully present being to any situation, the more you will have to share. Ask yourself what stands between you and really being present.

Not only do we have a tendency to be on autopilot, but we also arrive with our filters wherever we go. Our filters are from the past, and once we have had an experience with something or someone, that usually colours our experience in the present moment. We tend to be guided by old assumptions and unquestioned beliefs but are usually completely unaware of these filters. We probably all have someone in our business we have classified as a difficult colleague or annoying client. Most likely we dread those interactions, and during them we will look for any proof that confirms our preconceived ideas about the person.

This is nicely illustrated in the following Zen story: there was a person relocating to a new village and he was wondering if he would like it there, so he went to the local Zen master and asked, 'Do you think I will like it in this village? Are the people nice?'

The master asked back, 'How were the people in the town where you just came from?' 'They were nasty and greedy, they were angry and lived for cheating and stealing,' said the newcomer. 'Those are exactly the type of people we have in this village,' said the Zen master.

Shortly after that, another newcomer to the village visited the Zen master and asked the same question, to which the master asked, 'How were the people in the town where you come from?'

'They were sweet and lived in harmony, they cared for one another and for the land, they respected each other and they were seekers of spirit,' he replied. And the Zen master answered, 'Those are exactly the type of people we have in this village.'

The more mindful we become, the more present we become. The more present we are, the more we gain perspective, become aware of our filters and can meet each situation and person with an open mind.

Reflection on filters

The next time you walk into your office, imagine that you are walking into it for the very first time. What do you notice? Extend this exercise to meeting with a co-worker, client or subordinate that you regard as difficult: imagine that you are meeting them for the very first time. What do you notice?

5. Attention is a sought-after quality

Attention is a muscle that can be trained

We are living in an attention economy and a leader's ability to manage their attention is crucial when it comes to creativity and business success. Yet in our 24/7 always-on culture, distraction tends to be the norm and attention has become a sought-after quality. Given the many distractions leaders face, they need to actively train themselves to focus, and learn how to create space in their minds and schedules.

It is absolutely crucial for a leader to manage their attention.

Our brain has a capacity called neuroplasticity, which means it changes through behaviour. An indicator for neuroplasticity taking place in your brain is when you are initially trying to become proficient in a new skill and you experience a feeling of awkwardness, resistance or insecurity along the way. That feeling is an indicator that your brain is being shaped. Attention is a muscle that we can train through regular exercise. As such, mindfulness practice is widely referred to as exercise for the brain. Practising mindfulness is like going to the 'brain gym'. The only difference is that you don't actually have to go to a special location; your everyday life is your brain gym. Even though neuroscience is just at the beginning when it comes to learning about the effects of mindfulness practice on the brain, the results are encouraging. According to Professor Richard Davidson, 'given that our brains are constantly shaped wittingly or unwittingly – most of the time like a sailboat that lost its rudder in the middle of the ocean – we might as well start training our brains so that the boat sails in the direction we want it to' (Tlalka, 2016).

Tips for brain training

- It is not about emptying your mind or pushing thoughts away. It is normal for you to have thoughts during meditation as the mind secretes thoughts like the body secretes hormones.

- Whenever your mind wanders off to a thought, bring it back to your breath.

- The moment you notice your mind has wandered off is a moment to celebrate as you are already mindful.

Manage your distractions; don't be managed by them

There is no doubt that the digital age is challenging us both individually and collectively. We've already seen that our modern work-life environment is dominated by information overload, always-on connectivity, continual interruptions, and distractions through email and social media. Yet research says it is not technology itself that is stressing us out, but the addictive way in which we engage with it. Many research studies from reputable universities such as Harvard (Harvard Business Review Staff, 2013), Stanford (Gorlick, 2009) and others have been done on the disastrous effects of multitasking on our performance and productivity. What we commonly call multitasking is actually interrupting whatever we are doing in order to check our phones or devices. We are addicted to our devices and crave receiving new emails or social media alerts. The explanation for this is fairly simple: every time we check our emails, the pleasure centre in our brain receives a dopamine spike. Dopamine is an opioid, which is highly addictive. Studies show that we check our phones on average 85 times per day (Woollaston, 2015) and when we do, we essentially get the same effect as when a gambler makes a bet or a drug addict takes cocaine (Levitin, 2015). We often complain about information overload and distractions, but rather than asking whether emails are distracting us, the more pertinent question to ask is: How can we engage with email and our devices in a different and more skilful way?

Technology, the Internet and email were originally designed to connect us across wide distances and save us time for focusing on what is important to us. The availability of information at our fingertips can save us weeks of research, which means we could use this time to think about strategic problems, learn a new skill, be with our families, play a sport or meditate. Being able to check email anywhere, anytime can enable us to leave the office or travel without losing touch with our work. All of this is still true when we learn how to engage with email and social media in a more mindful and conscious way, instead of habitually and impulsively checking it all the time.

As we have seen, mindfulness does not require us to separate ourselves from our life, but invites us to engage with it in a different way. This includes the way we work and how we engage with our technology. As such, anything can become a mindfulness practice, even the way we engage with our emails.

When I work with senior leaders, I usually start by working on creating space in their minds and in their schedules. This usually includes questions about their email routine. What I found is that some of the most successful people that I meet make engaging and disengaging from the Internet a conscious choice. They tend to have dedicated times during their day when they check emails, and it is never the first thing they do in the morning. A business unit leader in a global industrial conglomerate told me:

> I never start my day with emails. At the beginning of the day is the time when my mind is the freshest; that's my thinking time. I don't need my mind to be fresh for answering emails. I do my emails at the end of the day, otherwise I will be a slave of everyone else's agenda.

So the next time, you feel an impulse to check your phone and interrupt your workflow or conversation with a co-worker, ask yourself if this is really what you would like to do in this particular moment or if it can wait and this was just the dopamine addiction kicking in.

As with any addictive or compulsive behaviour, the first step to change is usually to acknowledge the presence of addictive behaviour. Once the awareness is there, we can start to change something.

Neuroscientist professor Judson Brewer from Yale University has done some interesting research on how to stop our addiction to email and the Internet (Brewer, 2016). He suggests that the way we learn is through negative and positive reinforcement. As we are getting a dopamine spike in our brains when we check emails (even when they contain stressful messages), it is a positive reinforcement and our brain wants more of that. Brewer suggests applying a similar strategy to the one he used with smokers who had previously tried to quit smoking unsuccessfully at least five times. Unlike other programmes, which usually ask people to stop smoking, he encouraged the participants to smoke as much as they wanted to as long as they did it mindfully with full attention and curiosity. It turns out that smoking mindfully was extremely unpleasant and the success of his programme was twice as high as the normal gold standard therapeutic programmes for quitting smoking. Applied to our email addiction, this means that the next time you notice the urge to check your phone, just pause and bring curiosity to the experience. Where do you notice the urge? How does it feel? By bringing curiosity to the urge, we interrupt the automatic reactivity and create serotonin in our body, which counterbalances the addictive dopamine.

Reflection on email distraction

Over the course of this week, notice how often you are interrupting your workflow to check your phone or emails. You could also download the app Checky, which counts how often you check your phone.

Exercise for checking your emails as a mindfulness practice

Before you check your email, make a conscious choice as to whether you really want to check your emails at this time. Connecting and disconnecting from the Internet should be conscious acts. Once you open your inbox, observe your bodily sensations to a full inbox: do you hold your breath or tense up? As such, you can use checking your emails to create more awareness about potential stressors.

Exercise on limiting the use of social media

Use technology to limit the use of social media and emails. Experiment with switching off your email notifications and see what it does to your productivity. In addition, there are several apps that help you to monitor the use of social media, where you can limit how long and how often you can check it. Rather than fighting with your impulse to check your emails 30 times per hour, use technology to limit your Internet usage. Try out free apps such as Nanny for Google, StayFocusd, SelfControl or ColdTurkey.

6. Leaders are not paid to be busy

We live in a business culture where 'are you busy?' has become the new 'how are you?' Many executives carry a somewhat false pride of being busy, as they equate being busy with being important and it determines their self-value. The reality for many leaders is that they find themselves with a diary of back-to-back meetings, which is often matched by an even fuller inbox. Yet as a leader you are not paid to be busy. You are paid to think, create a vision for the business and inspire others to make this vision a reality.

In my coaching work, I usually start with helping clients to create more mental space, which includes a hard look at their diaries and how they structure their days.

When one of my clients, a partner in an investment firm, initially looked at his schedule, his days were just full of meetings. We went through them one by one and in his case it turned out that the majority of meetings in his diary were with people who wanted something from him. They were with brokers, headhunters, corporate finance firms, strategy consulting firms and so on. Most of them tried to build a relationship with him in order to sell him future services; yet they did not add any value to his priorities in the present. He did not want to have these meetings, but there was a feeling of not wanting to be impolite as he knew many of them. As a result, he had the meetings but crumbled inside and was not really present during them. It turned out that he had such an aversion against those meetings that he would subsequently give the work to other companies instead. As a result, he instructed his PA to clear these meetings from his schedule and only accept meeting invitations if they fitted with his priorities. He also began never having meetings before 10 am. This extra time enabled him to structure his day, and think about strategic issues regarding current portfolio companies or future deals. The result was that he felt much more satisfaction on the job.

I also worked with a start-up founder who at one point was annoyed when his team told him that they had too much to do and were too busy all the time. He came up with the idea that you could finish most tasks in 20 minutes if you worked in a focused way without interruptions. He put his idea to the test by timing himself with the help of the e.ggtimer.com website. He set himself 20-minute intervals, switched off email notifications and social media alerts and did this for a week. Not only was he able to finish every task in these 20-minute intervals, but he also found himself with two to three extra hours each day, which he could use to think about strategic issues. Needless to say, he has made this his regular style of working.

Tips for creating mind space

It is crucial for leaders to manage their distractions and carve out time and space to think.

- Instead of starting your day with emails or meetings, carve out some space in the morning for strategic work.
- Start your day with 'Mind Space Pages' instead of reactively responding to your inbox. This practice starts by writing

down everything that is on your mind in terms of things you need to do. This will clear your mental space and free up mental capacity to focus.

- Write down everything from scheduling a meeting to strategically thinking about events to booking a flight or paying a bill – literally everything that is on your mind that you need to do, however small.

- Look at the list again and group the items into small tasks and big tasks as well as online/offline tasks.

- Structure your day in a way that you can carve out one- to three-hour slots, where you focus on the big offline tasks.

- Don't check your emails all the time, but instead clear your inbox during dedicated time periods and use the time in between to work offline.

- Take a brief break approximately every 90 minutes. During the break go for a walk in the building/outside, take a few breaths or take a nap (15 minutes of sleep during the day are as effective as 2 hours of deep sleep at night), but don't surf the Internet as this further exhausts your brain.

- Use e.g.ggtimer.com to structure your day into 15/30/90-minute slots.

- Do several of the small tasks, which each only require a few minutes, during dedicated time periods (25–50 minutes). For most people, this is best done in the afternoon between 3 pm and 5 pm during low energy periods.

- Have a careful look at your diary and decide whether you really need to take every meeting that is scheduled or if you could send a team member instead.

Our chief want is someone who will inspire
us to be what we know we could be.

Ralph Waldo Emerson

7. Leadership presence as a key leadership skill

Leadership presence is something that we all recognise but it is often hard to put our finger on what it really is. Over the years I have met and interviewed thousands of very successful senior executives and while almost everyone displayed confidence and many were highly articulate, only a handful had what I would call leadership presence. Leadership presence or charisma does not automatically come with success or a job title, but is something that someone emanates with all of his or her being. It is a mix of how someone carries themselves, how they affect others and how they communicate verbally and non-verbally.

On the other hand, I have met people, particularly in Asia, who were poor and did quite simple support jobs, but whose presence commanded authority. When I lived in Hong Kong, there was a tiny lady in her sixties who would come every evening to clear out the garbage in our apartment building. She always radiated an inner peace and joy, and the quality of her presence charmed me and commanded my attention.

From my experience, one of the things that stands in the way of leadership presence is that many executives live mostly in their heads. Earlier in my career, before practising meditation and yoga on a regular basis, I used to be what I would call a 'fleeting head', pretty much only living from the neck up. I was completely absorbed in my thinking mind and relatively oblivious to what was happening in my body below the neck. I was not in touch with my 'beingness'.

When it comes to leadership presence, we can learn a lot from actors and start by fully inhabiting our whole bodies. If we think of actors before a performance, they would never come on stage without warming up their body extensively. They tend to be very much in tune with their bodies, aware of subtle signals like tightness or pressure. Actors also do breathing exercises to calm down their nervous system and manage their nerves before a performance.

Yet as leaders, we so often give talks and speak to our teams without ever checking in with our bodies. Leadership presence starts with our posture. Sensing into our posture and sensing the animating life force that energises the physical form creates presence.

Exercise to tune into presence

Take three, deep breaths. Then extend your arms and try sensing into the palms of your hands. Notice any sensations, such as temperature, blood flow and tingling, and notice the innate sense of aliveness in your palms.

Exercise to inhabit your space

This exercise can be done either standing or sitting down. Take a moment to notice your posture. Are your feet firmly grounded on the floor? Are you fully inhabiting and owning the space you occupy either sitting or standing? If you are not, imagine yourself to be standing firmly grounded and unshakeable like a mountain. Notice how your feet are making contact with the floor and any sensations that might be present in the soles of your feet. Use your breath to relax your body.

The other key ingredient for leadership presence is authenticity. Leading from an authentic place is offering to others a part of you that inspires. In order to have this heart-to-heart connection with others, a leader needs to have self-awareness. This means that you have to know yourself first and your values, but it also includes vulnerability. Very often leaders think they need to be one person at work and another person in private. They feel that they have to play a role when they are at work. The more senior you get in an organisation, the lonelier it can become, and many leaders feel that they need to portray themselves as strong and invincible. In my experience, particularly high-achievers have a tendency to try to be perfect, which allows no room for mistakes or vulnerability. As a result, many leaders live in quiet fear of making mistakes and try to control everything around them. They try to appear invincible, try to hide every perceived weakness, and in the process they often appear controlled, cold and unreachable to the people they are leading.

Mindfulness creates authenticity. When we face ourselves during meditation practice, we will inevitably also come up against our shadow sides and will learn how to accept them. As such, mindfulness practice contributes to making us more authentic. Langer has done some fascinating research on how being mindful increased the charisma and authenticity of female leaders (Bailey, 2015). Female leaders often have the problem that they are either seen as too soft if they behave like women or as too tough and scary if they behave more like men. Research experiments were performed with women who were instructed to behave either male-like or female-like and half of each group was instructed to be mindful. The result of this research experiment was that as long as the women acted mindfully, they were seen as more trustworthy, charismatic and authentic.

Reflection on leadership qualities

1. Make a list of all the leaders you admire and think of the qualities that they display. Often people who come to mind are Nelson Mandela, Maya Angelou, the Dalai Lama and Gandhi.

2. Make a second list of all the people who have influenced you in your life, including teachers, coaches, guides, parents and so on.

3. Reflect on the qualities that the people in both lists have. One of the things they will most likely have in common is that you experience a sense of command radiating from their inner, authentic presence.

4. Pick one quality that these leaders have and imagine how your life would be different if you emanated this quality. Imagine how your relationship with your chairman, peers, subordinates and customers would be different if you would display this quality. Imagine how your decision-making would be different. You can extend this reflection into your personal life as well to include your family.

Draw a Mind Map or use this circle to complete number 4 of the exercise on the previous page.

Figure 2 Reflection on leadership qualities

Between stimulus and response, there is a space.

Viktor Frankl

Part III
Managing others

A large portion of a leader's day is spent with people management.

Mindful leaders lead from the inside out and create and hold the space for others to shine. Instead of creating a climate of fear and leading in a command and control style, they create purpose-driven cultures, which encourage open communication and empower their people to access their full potential.

A leader's job is not to do the best job on each individual task or to know each individual area better than anyone else. A leader's role is more similar to the conductor of an orchestra: develop a vision, orchestrate people around a common purpose and create the space in which each and every one can flourish and accelerate their skills to the benefit of the greater advancement of all.

Micromanaging and letting go are often problems for high achievers as they are usually promoted for being the best at what they do in their individual area. It is a balancing act at first of trusting someone else to do as good a job as you did. But ultimately that's precisely what a leader needs to do, otherwise he or she ends up stifling the team's creativity and is actually not doing the job he or she has to do. One plus one is greater than two when it comes to working together with others. The skills of a team or group of people are always better than the individual qualities added together as they are creating something new when they work together. It is then the leader's role to foster the conditions for individual players to shine and to collaborate.

We've seen already that EQ is a prerequisite for being successful as a leader. In the relational field, the two things that trip us up are either negative thoughts or negative emotions. Self-awareness lies at the heart of EQ and is the first step to self-mastery. Mindfulness helps us to manage our nervous system and allows us to operate from a place of centredness. It is about reprogramming our nervous system by counteracting the tendencies in our mind that drive fear-based behaviour. According to the Dalai Lama, 'we need to transform our own minds – weaken the pull of our destructive emotions and so strengthen our better natures. This inner shift prepares us to enact a larger mission with clarity, calm and caring' (Goleman, 2015a).

Self-mastery is the starting point for managing others.

Most leaders that I work with are familiar with Daniel Goleman's four-quadrant EQ model. In Figure 3, I have recreated my version of this – the four-quadrant mindful leadership model.

Figure 3 The four-quadrant mindful leadership model

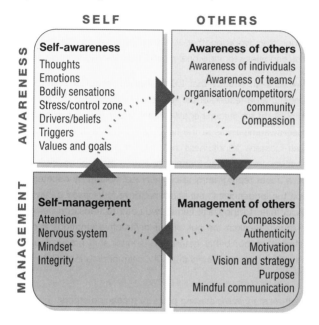

When we look at the four-quadrant mindful leadership model, we find awareness of others and management of others on the right side. Our awareness of others in the upper right quadrant includes awareness of the environment and what is going on with other people. This includes their storylines, motives, feelings, body language and what they care about. Research in neuroscience suggests that mindfulness training also strengthens the parts of the brain that are responsible for self-empathy and empathy for others, context sensitivity and social intuition (Begley and Davidson, 2012). Becoming more aware of others and caring more about them enables leaders to be more skilful people managers.

When it comes to effectively managing others (lower right quadrant), presence, authenticity and compassion are key. My experience with senior leaders has taught me that those leaders who care about the people they are leading and cooperating with are usually the wiser, more charismatic and effective leaders.

Integrating mindfulness into the leadership model adds presence, awareness and compassion. While many leaders are already aware of some of their habitual tendencies, the intellectual awareness is usually not enough to change unskilful behaviour. Leaders are often stuck in recurring behavioural patterns that have an undesired impact on the teams and organisations they are leading. That is precisely where mindfulness comes in. If a leader is present in the heat of the moment and notices that he or she is triggered, then there is a choice to do something different and stop the unskilful behaviour for the greater benefit of all.

When I speak to people about their stressors, people stress is usually the one that comes up the most often. This can be a colleague, a boss, a subordinate or a family member. In these moments, our solo practice is really put to the test and it is key to bring the same awareness to our interactions with others that we cultivate with ourselves during our individual mindfulness practice.

8. Authenticity builds trust and rapport

As we have seen, leading from an authentic place is offering to others a part of you that inspires. What creates trust with others is 'humanness': this includes honesty and a level of vulnerability. What doesn't create trust is trying to be perfect and portraying yourself as strong and invincible.

We tend to leave our personal emotional selves at home and play a certain role while we are at work. This often includes pretending to know the answer even when we don't know. As a CEO, it is important to become good at not knowing, letting the teams who do know do the work. You do not need to know all the answers, particularly in situations where you are dealing with the unknown. In those situations, it can be much more inspiring to name your concerns instead of pretending you have all the answers, painting the picture rosier than it is or playing a problem down.

We have probably all been at the receiving end of a speech by a senior leader that, while brilliantly written, failed to touch us, or in some cases even put us off and created more distance than connection between us and the speaker. It is often not so much about the content of what is shared but how it is shared. People generally can sense if something is off or not authentic.

One of my clients recently used the analogy of someone who is having an affair: 'Even though he or she might be saying all the right things and be physically present, one notices that his or her heart is not really in it and that he or she is somewhat absent.' Leaders can say all the right things but employees sense if someone's heart is not in it or if they are not truthful.

On the other hand it can be really powerful and a relief if a leader is transparent about what is going on. We previously discussed that awareness gives us a choice of how we want to respond to a situation, instead of reacting to it habitually and unconsciously. The same is true for a team or an organisation – after all, a team or an organisation is a group of people. As we have seen in times of uncertainty or when we are faced with the unknown, the mind has a tendency to create worst-case scenarios, which are often much worse than the reality we are facing. If we pretend that there is no problem, some of the organisation's energy will go to worrying about the future, including portraying worst-case scenarios, and people will try to make sense of the mixed messages they are receiving. As a result, valuable time and energy will be wasted in gossiping about the potential outcomes of a situation. Once the truth is out in the open and there is awareness about the situation, people can respond much more skilfully. There is an old saying that the devil you know is better than the devil you don't know. If a leader comes from a vibration of fear, it invites other people into that field and they are affected. Once a leader says that he or she is scared, everyone relaxes as they can see that the leader sees reality. It also allows people to openly acknowledge their own fears, and once all of this is in the open, the organisation can move on with the task at hand instead of being stifled by rumours and supposition.

Reflection on building trust

Take a moment to reflect on a situation where you were inspired by a leader's words. Then take a moment to reflect on a speech that left you feeling disconnected. What qualities were displayed in both situations?

Reflection on transparency

When you need to convey a difficult truth, what is your natural course of action? Are you usually playing a situation down or do you paint the picture rosier than it is? Or are you transparent about the situation and share your concerns? If you are not transparent in those moments, what is holding you back?

I've learned that people will forget what you said, people will forget what you did, but people will never forget how you made them feel.

Maya Angelou

9. Mastering communication

We are always communicating in one way or another, willingly or unwillingly, even if we don't say a word. Like a mobile phone, our brain has a transmitter and a receiver and we have wireless connections with other people's brains. We are continually sending and receiving information. When we communicate with each other, auditory and visual signals are processed by social synapses in our brains. Professor Joy Hirsch at Yale has done some fascinating research in this area, which suggests that when two brains communicate they literally work as one, provided that the two people give each other their full attention (euronews, 2015). Yet it has become rare in today's 24/7 attention economy, with all its internal and external distractions, that we give someone our full attention. While it used to be a faux pas to answer your phone during a meeting or at the dinner table, it has unfortunately become more of a norm than an exception to check emails or social media updates while in conversation with someone else. While we read emails, we continue nodding or making some sounds of appreciation or agreement, but actually only listen to parts of the conversation and often miss the most essential details. As a result, two parties can have a conversation and think they agreed on something, while they actually have not understood each other at all. We are so used to having half-hearted conversations like this that we no longer tell each other off. It sometimes takes a young child or a grandparent to point out to us that we are not fully listening to them.

Our mobile devices are not the only distraction that can capture our attention. Attention can also be hijacked by our mind's tendency to wander off into the future or worry about the past. Generally, the more emotional charge an event or a thought has for us, the more it is likely that we are pulled into thoughts. If we notice that we are distracted and in that moment open up and apologise and say we were not listening, that can change the dynamic entirely.

And then there are the people who just use listening as waiting time until it is their turn to speak. Have you ever had a conversation with someone who interrupts you and finishes your sentences as they think they already know what you are going to say next? My partner sometimes has that tendency as he feels he has a very quick mind. Yet when I speak from a place of centredness and presence, even I don't know what I will be saying next. Consequently, in those moments, the conversation falls short of its potential of creating real connection, deep understanding and learning.

It is important to point out that hearing is not the same as listening. While hearing is automatic and unconscious and we can't really stop ourselves from hearing, listening is a conscious and mental effort. Listening requires full attention on what is said, including not just listening to someone's words but also taking in facial expressions, body language and gestures. This is one of the reasons why people often misunderstand each other when they have conversations by text, email or instant messaging. Another barrier to listening is our internal storylines or filters. Often we come to a situation and listen either in a defensive way or we just try to confirm our own hypothesis. Effective listening then also includes being aware of your 'listening filters', which include a closed mindset and precognitive commitment fixed on previously-formed opinions on a particular subject.

Culture is usually built from the top. If a leader does not listen well, that usually sets an example for the rest of the organisation.

Reflection on good conversations

Think of the last time you felt that someone really listened to you, where you felt truly heard. What did the person do and how did you feel? Then think of a conversation where you did not feel heard, maybe someone interrupted you, finished your sentences, was texting while you spoke or responded with saying something about their own situation or with something entirely unrelated to what you had just said. How did you feel and how did this affect the connection and trust that was created?

The persuasive power of listening

Most leaders I speak to consider themselves good listeners. Yet, from my experience, many leaders are just hearing in order to respond when they should be listening to understand. Jeff Immelt, GE's CEO, has described listening, whether it is to customers, employees or others who may affect the business, as 'the single most undervalued and under-developed business skill' (Clegg, 2014). The International Listening Association (listen.org) lists over 35 studies that indicate listening as a top skill needed for business (yes, I was surprised, too, that there is a society for listening). Listening is so important, as when we listen, we learn what motivates others and it is much easier to build trust, influence and gain buy-in for an idea or to sell.

One of the things I learned early on as a headhunter was that the only way to get someone to the table was to listen to them first. It was key to make them talk about what they liked and disliked about their current role and to hear about their desired next move. Learning about these things enabled me to pitch the role I was recruiting for in the light of their needs or desires, which made the conversation very easy. On the flip side, we have probably all been at the receiving end of a sales conversation where someone just launched into a sales pitch without even knowing our background and without noticing how we tensed up and our body language changed. And most likely we will not have bought what was on offer unless we bought it only to get rid of the salesperson as quickly as possible. The quiet art of listening is often the most underdeveloped skill when it comes to leadership.

Yet attentive listening is one of the most powerful tools when it comes to building trust and rapport with others. Giving someone your full attention is so powerful, as it makes people feel safe to open up about what is really on their mind.

We are living in a time where self-promotion on social media is at an all-time high. As a result, we can easily get the impression that whoever shouts the loudest is the most convincing. Yet researchers from Columbia Business School found that the quiet art of listening is equally as important as being articulate when it comes to persuasion (Ames et al., 2012).

Having interviewed a few hundred if not over 1,000 senior executives during my time as a headhunter, I would like to share two examples of highly persuasive communicators, which might come as a surprise.

It was in 2011 and I was recruiting for the CEO role of an Asian infrastructure company, which was jointly owned by Chinese and American private equity investors. The selection committee was composed of two interviewers from each side. It took all day to interview the six short-listed candidates and by 7 pm the panel started their evaluation. Until about 10 pm it was mostly a discussion between the two American partners, which was going around in circles, while the two Chinese investors were completely silent. I remember at the time being a bit perplexed by the sheer lack of contribution from the Chinese side and I must admit I initially underestimated them. At 10 pm there was a moment of longer silence. In that moment, one of the Chinese investors asked a simple and clear question, which summed up what was said and cut right to the chase. We found a solution 20 minutes later and the committee agreed on a final candidate.

The other example I would like to share with you was when I was building an Asia advisory board for a global luxury company. The nature of the business meant that the CEO had direct access to Hollywood actors, the most successful entrepreneurs, CEOs, philanthropists and politicians around the globe. One of the potential board members I introduced to him was a female Chinese executive in her early sixties, a regional CEO, who had an impressive background but was slightly less experienced on an international scale compared to some of the other candidates. After the meeting, my client told me that this was the most impressive person he had met in the past ten years. I was a bit surprised at the time and asked him what it was that impressed him so much. He commented that he had never met anyone who listened so intently and quietly yet with so much presence and authority. He said that she did not say much, but what she said and the questions she asked were spot on and highly intelligent.

Exercise 1: to hone your listening skills

Every time you have a meeting, try your best to keep your full attention on the speaker. If you notice your mind wandering off into the past, the future or to comment on what you are listening to, just bring your attention back to the speaker. Most likely you will have to repeat this over and over again. Notice whether you have a tendency to interrupt the other person or an urge to share your own impressive story. Also notice any assumptions you are making.

Mindful communication

Mindful communication means to listen and speak with awareness and compassion. It is about bringing the same non-judgmental awareness and presence to our conversations that we bring to our own meditation practice. In many ways it is the advanced version of our solo practice. It helps us to become more aware of our mind and mental habits during conversations. Mindful communication has two parts and includes the way we listen and the way we speak. It requires us to give someone else our full attention. We are asked to interrupt our automatic pilot and to stop and notice what is present right now. In that moment, we go back to that space of centredness and we can listen to someone with our full being rather than just with our mind's filters. In a similar way, when we drop into the space of not knowing before we speak, we reconnect with our innate wisdom. This can help us to find solutions in situations where we are stuck and whatever we say has authenticity.

Instructions for mindful communication

Pause

Interrupt whatever you were doing and pause for a moment.

Drop into the space of not knowing

Take a few breaths or become aware of the sensations in your palms to fully arrive in the present moment. Try to drop your ideas about the situation and to be open and curious.

Listen deeply

If you are the listener, give your full attention to the speaker, resisting any urge to interrupt or comment. If your mind wanders off, just bring it back. As the speaker, notice what is present right now and allow your thoughts to emerge instead of rushing to speak. Try to be comfortable with a moment of silence.

Speak your truth with compassion

Rather than saying what you think the other person would like to hear, speak your own truth, but do it with compassion and kindness.

Managing difficult conversations

As a leader, having difficult conversations is part of the daily bread and butter. These can include difficult conversations with a board member, peer, subordinate, customer, supplier, competitor or the media.

What difficult conversations tend to have in common is that there is either some kind of expected confrontation or we have an agenda to get a certain point across. Generally we try to get something from the conversation, which we either do not receive from the other person or we are concerned that we might not be getting what we want. We all have people in our professional lives that we have labelled as difficult or unpleasant or even as our enemy. Most likely every interaction we have with them reinforces this opinion, as we are habitually focusing on any signs of difficulty or unpleasantness, and continually reinforcing our perception. From my experience, most people are defensive when they are getting negative feedback and that is true for leaders as well. These are the moments where we risk getting into our stress zone and become defensive or closed and often it is precisely that which gives us the unwanted result.

In those moments it is crucial to cultivate mindful awareness.

I vividly remember the first time I had to give someone feedback about their annual appraisal. Our company had prepared a short video on how to handle difficult conversations and give feedback to someone who was rated lower than they expected. I felt mentally prepared for the conversation, yet when I was in it, I was surprised by the intensity of active resistance that I received, agitated and triggered. After a while I noticed that my body started tensing as well and I used this body awareness to stay in my control zone and remain calm in the situation.

As we have seen, increased self-awareness includes being aware of when we as leaders are triggered and start blaming others or become closed and defensive. It allows us to see if we are making assumptions or if negative emotions are triggered. When we own these feelings and have a sense of how they may relate to our own un-met underlying needs, we can move away from projective and reactive blaming and move back to reflective focus where we can drop back into not knowing and being open. In those moments we can get back in touch with what is really going on and, as such, respond in a wiser way that is more effective. If we have this type of awareness, we can practise mindfulness of breathing or ask for a break to leave the room to get back to a place of centredness before we say anything from a triggered place that we will regret later on.

Reflection on difficult conversations

Start by reflecting on a difficult conversation that you've had in the past two weeks. Why was the conversation difficult? What did you expect to receive and what did you receive from the other person?

Reflection on habitual ways of relating

Do you have any habitual ways of reacting to certain people? If the answer is yes, what are the underlying stories and assumptions that you have about them? Ask yourself if they are really true.

Exercise 1: on taking someone else's perspective

Think about a difficult conversation that you've recently had with a peer, employee or your board, then put yourself completely into the other party's shoes. Try your best to make the argument from the other person's point of view, which includes technically arguing the other person's argument. Really try to get under their skin and argue their case.

Exercise 2: on taking someone else's perspective

Think about topics or people you don't like. Then pick one of them and try your best to find at least three things that another person might find positive and interesting about it/them.

Getting buy-in from key stakeholders

The more senior we get in an organisation, the more we are required to get buy-in from key stakeholders. This could be the board, our employees, shareholders, suppliers or the community. Driving change, in particular, always requires getting buy-in from key stakeholders both inside and outside an organisation. Often this includes dealing with opposing views. When there are opposing views, it is quite easy to have an 'us versus them' mentality. We might even see other people as an 'enemy' that stands in our way; we forget that we are all interconnected. In a scenario like that, nobody can win. It is important to remain open and to come back to the centred space, where we are not acting in a fear-based, caveman way. We have to come back to the space of not knowing where we can remain curious and ask questions again and again, which allows us to appreciate our common humanness and what everybody brings to the table. This allows us, in the case of opposing views, to find a solution with which everyone can live. It may not be 100 per cent of what each party wants, but if we can get everyone more comfortable with these grey areas, much more is achieved.

Earlier in this chapter, we discovered that attentive listening is one of the most powerful tools when it comes to building trust and rapport with others. The more we listen and the more we understand where someone else is coming from, the easier it is to find common ground and get buy-in from the other party. In a board, for example, what is required is harmony. As a board is just a group of people, the individual need for being heard and seen is equally applicable here. Yet every so often we don't know what others think of us and we are hesitant to ask for feedback.

One of the cardinal mistakes that many leaders make when they are new to a role or organisation is an eagerness for 'showing off' their knowledge or sharing their opinions before they listen. As an executive coach, I often work with newly-promoted high potentials or leaders who have been appointed to a role from outside an organisation. Most companies have on-boarding programmes, which usually involve a variety of meetings across different levels and functional areas within an organisation. In these situations, there is a natural inclination of wanting to impress others or prove our value, which often includes an eagerness for sharing our knowledge. As a result, there is often a tendency to speak more than to listen. So one of the things that I instruct my coaching clients to do is to use these meetings to learn, ask open questions and to listen much more than they speak. By following this advice, these meetings can be used for learning about an organisation and the motivation of each individual they meet. They can be used for building trust and getting buy-in, which is crucial for driving informed change later on.

Reflection on getting buy-in

Take a moment to think about the people you are meeting. What do they care about? What do they need in order to feel that they have been heard and seen? How can you find common ground?

Exercise 2: to hone your listening skills

The next time you have a meeting, try to give your full attention to the other person. Try to be curious about what they are saying to you. When they stop talking, ask them an open question, such as 'tell me more about that' and resist the urge to immediately share your opinion.

Meditation for cultivating compassion

We can train ourselves to be more compassionate with loving kindness meditation.

Follow this link to a five-minute loving kindness meditation: palmamichel.com/breathing-meditation/

10. Getting the most out of your team

Leaders need to create a learning container, which allows their team to shine. We've already discovered that speaking your truth with compassion and listening are key when it comes to building trust and rapport with the people you are leading. Particularly when the going gets tough, a leader's mindset and behaviour is key to keep the team motivated.

Mindset matters

Focus the team on the bigger picture

The mindset of a leader can play a crucial role when it comes to motivating or demotivating a team. I recently had a conversation with the CEO of a logistics business and he said that, from his experience, there are leaders who are 'energy suckers' and leaders who are 'energisers'. What he meant was that some people tend to focus only on the negative and point out all the things that are wrong in a business. Don't get me wrong, it is a crucial skill, particularly in a change management scenario or restructuring, if someone can point out what isn't working in a business. It is more about the way this is presented. Another way of presenting uncomfortable truth is to point out what needs fixing, but to put this into the context of the bigger picture and relate it to the new and positive things that will be created.

Our mind has a negativity bias, which means there is a natural tendency to focus on the things that are not working (Marano, 2003). As you are reading this, there is generally more right with your life than wrong with your life. Yet we have probably all experienced that whenever we are having a problem with one person at work or one of our projects is in trouble, this tends to overshadow everything else. Even if 99 per cent of someone's day was great, we tend to zoom in on the 1 per cent that wasn't.

In particular, perfectionists have a tendency only to point out when someone has made a mistake rather than also acknowledging what works well: this can be hugely demotivating for employees. A little bit of praise for things well done can go a long way as everybody has an underlying need for approval.

As a leader, it is important to be able to point the team back to the bigger picture. It is about reminding the team, yes, the present is unpleasant but it is part of a bigger picture. Rather than getting hung up only on the negative, it is about formulating a realistic but positive outlook. A leader needs to be able to address individual problems, but also be able to have a helicopter view at the same time. This is where the mindfulness practice comes in. When we meditate we gain insight and the ability to step back and see the bigger picture.

Use mindset as motivator

The mindset of a leader and of individual team members can have a huge impact, which is powerfully illustrated in the following two stories.

The first example is the breaking of the record of the four-minute mile. Until 1954, it was widely believed that it was not possible for human beings to run a mile under four minutes. This was until Roger Bannister proved people wrong by breaking the record in that year. Even more remarkable than him breaking the record was that, shortly after, a few other people broke the record as well. One of the key moments that led to his success was that Bannister came closer and closer to the four-minute mark. Unlike others who believed it was not possible, he believed that it was within reach.

The second example comes from Langer, with Alia Crum, who conducted an experiment with 84 chambermaids in New York (Spiegal, 2008). She divided them into two groups. Initially both were examined by doctors in terms of overall health and fitness level, including measuring their weight and body mass index (BMI). One group was told that what they were doing every day was like going to the gym and the other group was not given that information. After a month, they brought both groups together again and the doctors re-examined them. The results were astonishing: not only did the group that was told that they did exercise all day look much younger, they had also lost weight and their BMI had dropped.

There is quite a bit of research on the power of appreciation from reputable universities, such as the University of California, Berkeley (Greater Good, n.d.). The meaning of the word appreciation is interesting as it does not only mean being grateful but also augmenting in value. Whatever we focus our attention on grows. Research from the leading positive psychology researcher Barbara Fredrickson (2003) from the University of North Carolina at Chapel Hill also shows that emotions have a spiralling effect, meaning that the emotion we are having in this moment directly affects the emotion in the next moment. As such, appreciation practice has a cumulative effect. In challenging times it is easy to get bogged down by the negatives, but as a leader it is your responsibility not to lose sight of the broader picture and help the team focus on the positive.

Reflection on shifting your perspective

Just pause here for a moment and think of the two examples of the four-minute mile and the chambermaid study. Think about a project at work where your team is stuck or where you feel that something is not possible. What could you do to shift perspective?

Appreciation exercise

Write down five things that you appreciate about your company, your team and your industry. Include small things as well as bigger things. Repeat this every day for a month and see what happens.

Building connection through team meetings

There is quite a bit of research that highlights the importance of listening for leading teams and how damaging the lack of listening can be for team performance, employee engagement and motivation.

The VUCA world is not just affecting you as a leader but also each and everyone you lead. Employees want their voices to be heard. So the more you can listen to the people you are leading and learn about what they are thinking about and try to understand their concerns, the more you can build trust and the more successful you will be as a leader. It is not about becoming the chief psychologist of your organisation. What is required instead is a curiosity, care and interest in the people you are leading.

A powerful example for this type of listening comes from Dale Carnegie's all-time bestseller, *How to Win Friends and Influence*

People. He quoted a man, who described a meeting with Sigmund Freud:

> It struck me so feasibly that I shall never forget him. His eyes were mild and genial. His voice was low and kind. His gestures were few. The attention he gave me, his appreciation for what I said, even when I said it badly, was extraordinary. You have no idea what it meant to be listened to like that.

What this points to is the basic human need for connection and for being seen and heard. The best gift we can give to the people we lead is to offer them our full and undivided attention. This includes being open and caring about what they say instead of making meetings with the team just a tick-the-box type exercise.

Google recently embarked on a quest to find out what makes best-performing teams and what came up was psychological safety, which rests on equal turn taking in conversation and average social sensitivity, no one shutting the other people down and where different opinions are appreciated (Duhigg, 2016). The key then as a leader is to create an environment where everyone can participate and everyone's voice is heard, rather than one person dominating or shouting others down.

Team meetings are an excellent opportunity for checking in with the overall pulse of the team. They are opportunities for team building and for connecting and aligning around a common purpose. Yet team meetings are often dreaded and seen as a necessary evil.

Why is it that internal meetings so often fall short of their potential?

I recently had a conversation with a senior partner of a global consulting firm, who was about to go into an internal meeting, which he anticipated to be a bit of a waste of time. He then paused and said, 'I wonder if we prepared for internal meetings as well as we did for external meetings, they would be better.' We also spoke after his meeting and I asked him how it went. As expected, it was not very productive, which led him to this, 'What if our internal meetings were focused on team building rather than half-hearted attempts of getting us together around technical problems. I think we could probably walk away working much better together which would be fun.'

Internal meetings often lack preparation and focus. They tend to have too many people attend that do not have a clear role and they often take too long. It is unfortunately also fairly common that a leader waffles on and speaks much more than they listen.

When I was still working as a headhunter, I remember internal brainstorming meetings: a group from different functional areas would come together and one partner would share a role description with the group, while some people were tapping away or reading messages on their phones or were somewhere else within the confines of their minds. At the end of the meeting someone would usually say, 'This is great. Why don't you sum this all up in an email and I will send you some ideas.' In other words, the meeting did not solve the problem and did not do anything to form good working relationships.

One of the first things I encourage my corporate clients to do is to ban phones from meetings and start their team meetings with a quick check-in. This can be done with either just a moment of silence, which allows everyone to fully arrive in the room, or with bringing people together around a common question. It can be a personal check-in, asking about what is going on in their personal lives. Clients often report back that they might have felt negative about someone, but learning about what was going on in their life and feeling the common humanness created a huge shift.

Team meetings are an excellent opportunity for building connections if they emphasise sharing and are not dominated by just one person overshadowing everyone else. In general, people want to be heard and seen, yet often hide behind their roles and titles. An excellent way to break through the barriers of roles and responsibilities and build connection is to start the meetings with an open question instead of immediately jumping to technical issues. I encourage leaders to ask questions that, while related to work, go deeper and act as sort of a pulse check. By asking people, for example, what they are currently struggling with or if they have any concerns regarding one of the team's projects, people get pushed out of their comfort zone and can't hide behind technical knowledge. It is the leader's role to hold the space for the meeting and allow for equal turn taking, which creates connection between team members.

Reflection on team meetings

Take a moment to think about your last team meeting. Was there a clear agenda? Were people engaged? Did you leave the meeting feeling it had achieved what you intended it to?

Reflection on creating connection during team meetings

How could you create more connection between team members? What would be good questions to introduce to encourage sharing? How could you encourage equal turn taking between the meeting participants?

We cannot solve our problems with the same thinking we used when we created them.

Albert Einstein

11. Building a culture for innovation

Creativity and innovation are more than ever becoming distinguishing factors for success in our VUCA world, which requires us to think out of the box and operate in unknown territory. With the rise of artificial intelligence (AI) and many technical jobs soon to be replaced by robots, it is really our team's creativity and ability to innovate that sets us apart and will decide success or failure in the long run. As such, creativity and innovation need to rank high on the leadership agenda.

Rather than necessarily having to be the most creative person in the room, it is a leader's job to build a culture and an environment that is supportive for creativity and innovation. This stands and falls with the personality of the leader, as the culture usually starts from the top. You can put as many bean bags and ping pong tables into your office as you want, but if you are a perfectionistic control freak that is not open to change or shouts at people whenever they make a mistake, the best office design won't help to unlock your team's creative genius.

The space of not knowing

Creativity happens in the space of not knowing. It requires a space, an opening from which something new can arise.

Creativity is about making novel connections between what we know and what we don't know. It requires us to take a different perspective and it often involves walking on uncharted ground. As a leader, if you think you know all the answers or all there is to know about a situation, a product, an industry, your customer and so on, then you stop asking questions and become closed. There is little room for anything new to emerge and a risk of becoming complacent. It is a leader's job to allow and enable that space of openness and not knowing, which includes asking questions and allowing people the freedom to go away and experiment.

The creative process is a play between different states of mind. At times it requires complete openness to all sorts of different stimuli and allowing the mind to wander, and at other times it needs concentrated focus. It is also a play between our conscious mind, between everything that we know, and our unconscious mind, which continuously scans our environment for new input and has stored pretty much everything that we ever experienced without us having direct awareness of it. Sometimes we might have screened our conscious mind for an idea, spoken to all the experts and researched the Internet and all available resources that we can think of, but we are stuck and are going around in circles in our minds. In those moments, we can't force our subconscious brain to come up with creative ideas or find the solution on demand. Neuroscience shows that just before a creative insight, the brain rests in a relaxed alpha wave state. As a leader, you can use this knowledge in a meeting when you notice that your team is 'cooked' or stuck with a problem. If we continue in these moments with the meeting and think if we just push through that someone will have a creative spark, we are just wasting everyone's time. If we are stuck, but continue to think about the problem, our brain can't get into the alpha wave state and we block our subconscious mind from giving us those light-bulb moments when ideas bubble up to the surface. As counterintuitive as it might seem, in those moments we need to have a break or send the team members away to catch some sleep or do any other relaxing activity of their choice. This will more likely allow their brains to come up with novel ideas. In the broader scheme of things, we can use this knowledge to build a culture that lets teams go away and explore and expose themselves to all sorts of different inputs. Having said that, many organisations still have a 'bum on seat' type culture where face time is important. In those cultures, employees feel it would not be OK to put their head down to have a power nap or to take some time out for meditation or a walk around the block when they are stuck. Instead, they continue starring at their screens and only continue to exhaust their brains, which is counterproductive for creative output.

Collaboration is key

In today's business environment, there is a growing recognition that good ideas can come from anywhere and are not strictly linked to hierarchy, functional expertise or years of experience. There is also recognition that diversity of opinion, gender, race and age is crucial for innovation. Collaboration across functions and hierarchies is key when it comes to innovation, yet the reality in many companies is that there are independent silos that do not speak to each other. It is not enough to just tell employees to collaborate and speak with each other. As long as departments have their individual targets and reward structures, there is usually a clash of priorities. It is the leader's role to break down these silos and align people around a common purpose.

In addition, the best ideas often do not come from within companies but from nimbler start-ups. It can be beneficial to collaborate with or invest in start-ups or hire millennial whizz-kids. Having said that, if there is no openness in your company's culture, there will be a cultural clash and the collaboration will most likely fail.

Holding the creative container

More often than not, the creative process does not happen in a linear way, but in a spiral and we might have to take several U-turns. This means, we often move two steps forward and take one step backwards, before being catapulted to the next level of the spiral. This can sometimes be experienced as a bumpy ride and can often lead to resistance or demotivation in a team. In addition, when different people with different backgrounds, different agendas and potentially competing priorities come together, there is friction and potential for conflict. As discussed in Chapters 2 and 4, whenever there is uncertainty, we are dealing with the unknown or experience setbacks, there is a tendency for people to get triggered and into amygdala territory. It is the leader's job to be aware of this dynamic, keep himself or herself in the control zone and not lose sight of the bigger picture. In those moments, it is the leader's role to be able to stay with the discomfort of the situation and keep the process going. It is like being the captain of a sailboat in the middle of a storm, who needs to remain calm, centred and focused to sail the ship through the turmoil. When we sit in meditation, we become more and more familiar and comfortable with that space of not knowing. We gain awareness of when we or our team members are in their stress zones and, as such, gain the choice of getting back to this place of centredness again and again.

The challenge then for you as a leader is to help to create an environment that is supportive to awaken those states and qualities of mind that help your team's creativity to flourish, and to interrupt those states or qualities of mind that kill your team's creativity.

Common obstacles to creativity

- Stress, pressure, uncertainty
- Pushing too hard when we need to pause
- No time and space to think
- Being on autopilot
- No tolerance for failure
- Results over process orientation

As we have touched on how mindfulness is supportive with most of these issues in earlier chapters, I would like to particularly hone in on fear of failure and a results over process orientation. Both are interlinked to me.

Whenever we are walking on uncharted ground, we are bound to make mistakes. In addition to that, practice makes perfect. If you have ever learned a new skill, for example riding a bike, you probably painfully remember how many times you fell off before you managed to ride the bike successfully for the first time. In the same way, when we are creating something new we need to be able to experiment and try out different things in order to create a perfect product. Similarly, if you control the creative process too tightly, there is no freedom for anything unexpected to arise. Sometimes it can be precisely an unexpected mash-up that gives root to creativity as it shakes up our normal way of thinking.

I would like to pause here and reflect on the notion of failure by using Google Glass as an example: take a moment to think about Google Glass. In your mind was it a success or a failure? Looking at it from a single product perspective in terms of commercial success, it was a spectacular failure. Looking at it in the wider context, it was one of the first wearable tech products and allowed Google to gain knowledge and valuable insight for different uses of the technology and later product developments such as Google's smart contact lens. From this perspective, I would consider it an overall success.

The other example I would like to share comes from the fashion industry. These days designers are required to come up with collections for six selling seasons per year and are under tremendous pressure to produce creative ideas on demand 'right now' or better yesterday. I spoke to several creative directors of global fashion labels and one of them told me that rather than seeing individual collections, he sees a continuous creative process and whatever he does not perfect in one collection, he can use in the next collection.

It is also widely known that the famous Post-it® note was a by-product of the process of inventing a superglue, which of course wasn't a success.

These stories should encourage you to allow failure in your organisation. If a culture has a no failure policy, this can lead to fear of failure, which tends to alert an employee's amygdala, and can lead to creative paralysis or procrastination. In addition, there can also be a tendency to hide mistakes or only communicate them at a stage when it is too late to prevent larger damage. Having said that, it is important to remain interested in the process and continue to ask questions during it and not just afterwards. This can include holding not just a post-mortem on a project failure, but also a pre-mortem to think through all the different reasons why a project could potentially fail. Practising mindfulness naturally instils a process rather than an outcome orientation and the ability to be calm in the face of adversity.

When we practise mindfulness, our focus is on our experience in the present moment without being fixed on a particular outcome, and we bring curiosity to this experience. As such, we are cultivating our ability to focus on the process rather than on an isolated outcome.

Reflection on failure

Just take a moment and think about your company's creative process. Is there room for failure? Are projects seen in isolation or are they part of a continual creative process?

Reflection on difficult moments during the creative process

What do you as a leader do when the team gets stuck? What do you do when there is friction between team members or conflicting agendas?

Reflection on culture

Is your current culture supportive for creativity? Are there silos in your organisation? Is it possible for employees to take breaks or work from outside the office or does your culture require face time at one's desk?

All men are caught in an inescapable network of mutuality, tied in a single garment of destiny. Whatever affects one directly, affects all indirectly.

Martin Luther King

Part IV
Effecting broader change

Mindful leaders build mindful cultures, which are not purely driven by greed and competition but are more cooperative in nature and take into account the company's role in the broader system.

Every company has an impact on their customers and communities, and in today's global interconnected world that impact can be amplified. As a result, every leader must be aware of the potential impact that his or her actions can have on communities and the world at large. Leaders are asked to find harmony between the individual company interests with the interests of their customers, communities and the planet. They are required to step back and take a broader, more inclusive and cooperative perspective. However, this is easier said than done, particularly in times of economic pressure. Yet having an 'us versus them' mentality stands in direct contrast to our overall interconnectedness and can only backfire in the long run. As such, it is crucial to build companies that operate in a more collaborative and cooperative way. Leaders are required to notice when they are stuck in fear-based behaviour or a scarcity mindset and have lost sight of the bigger picture. As we have seen, mindfulness creates self-awareness and is a key that unlocks the door to openness, trust and collaboration. It allows leaders to stand back and listen more deeply to what is present, instead of getting lost in the heat of the moment.

In today's business environment, it is also more and more important for companies to have a positive purpose, which goes beyond simply making a profit and creating short-term value for its shareholders. According to Goleman, purpose acts as a powerful motivator:

> People feel part of a shared mission. This is quite meaningful: They have a shared common purpose. It makes work exciting, and it makes work engaging.
>
> Daniel Goleman, *The Executive Edge: An insider's guide to outstanding leadership*

This is also backed-up by a number of research studies (Kanter, 2011), which highlight that having a purpose motivates and mobilises employees and customers in a way that pursuing profits alone never will. It is particularly the generation of millennials that is less driven by finding a secure lifetime career but more attracted by contributing to a shared mission, a purpose that is bigger than them. In a time where people spend more and more time at work and our connectivity makes the boundaries between work and life more and more blurry, contributing to a bigger purpose goes a long way to motivate and attract employees. In order to act as a motivator or brand builder, this type of purpose needs to go beyond a mere mission statement, but has to be enacted through behaviour. It needs to be a lived reality, and intention and action need to be linked to the purpose. Some companies even go beyond that and help everyone in their company to try to find his or her own individual purpose.

Reflection on company purpose

Does your company have a positive purpose that goes beyond creating short-term shareholder value? If it does, is this purpose a lived reality and how does it show up in the organisation? If it doesn't, how could your company or team contribute to a bigger purpose?

Reflection on aligning action with purpose

When you take a strategic action, ask yourself why you are doing that and how is that aligned with your purpose? How are you embodying your purpose?

In order to carry a positive action we must
develop here a positive vision.

Dalai Lama

12. Sustainability – acting today for tomorrow

Sustainability is a topic that leaders can no longer ignore. Leaders are asked to build solutions now for a better future and we all have our part to play. Many companies are starting to look at better ways of balancing long-term goals over short-term gains. In today's interconnected world, this trend is partially driven by the rise in social media, which instantaneously connects companies and consumers and puts corporate behaviour and sustainability activities into the spotlight. There is a new breed of consumers, particularly the generation of millennials, which put a high emphasis on sustainability. Sustainability can be a trust builder and even driver for growth, but on the flip side, if something goes wrong, as seen with the recent Volkswagen scandal, a company's stock price and reputation can be impacted significantly. As such, sustainability needs to be part of every company's risk management. In addition, leaders recognise that they can no longer leave it solely to governments to tackle issues such as climate change or the declining of natural capital, but need to play an active role and make their contribution. One of the reasons is that leaders realise that their supply chain will simply disappear if they do not play their part when it comes to issues such as water shortage or deforestation. Every leader currently has a choice of contributing to building solutions for a better future or contributing to the further destruction of the planet. For a mindful leader, short-term thinking without considering the long-term impact and the overall consequences on the world around them is not an option. It is about creating a win–win situation for all parties in the long run.

To some of you, prioritising sustainability might sound like a hard ask in times of economic pressure. As humans, we normally tend to only react to dangers when they are immediate, as the amygdala motivates us to take action. Dangers that are more abstract and less immediate, such as climate change or a potential drying out of a supply chain, which won't happen in the immediate future, are not motivating us to take action in a similar way. Making a decision about producing our T-shirts in Bangladesh might sound like a good idea from a short-term production cost perspective, but the moment the factory collapses and there is an outcry of international media, the long-term effects on our brand and reputation heavily outweigh the short-term gains. Sustainability is not just a 'feel good' activity, but can have direct implications on the bottom line when actions and company activities are not sustainable. Many production and supplier processes were set up long before sustainability was a consideration. As a result, there might be looming sustainability risks in your current supply chain. It is particularly our interconnectedness and the power of social media that puts the spotlight on collapsing factories in Bangladesh or the recent Volkswagen scandal. In order to mitigate potential financial and reputational damage, leaders are required to increase the visibility in their supply chains and partner networks. This needs to be more than a tick-box exercise, and involves building collaborative networks, based on transparency and a common purpose, with suppliers and other partners.

As leaders, we are asked to make decisions all the time. What is important is the intention behind the decision and we are asked to question the sustainability of our thoughts and actions. This balancing act between short-term gains and long-term needs requires a leader to stop, stand back and see the bigger picture. It is only by taking this helicopter view that leaders will be able to decide on the best course of action now towards achieving a better future.

There are examples of bold leaders who make sustainability not just a tick-box exercise, but also a core part of their business strategy. One of these leaders is the CEO of Unilever, who changed the way Unilever reports business results in order to be able to make long-term issues like food security, deforestation and smallholder farming part of their business strategy. Other companies like Patagonia, Pukka or Bulb are registered B Corporations. B Corporation is a not-for-profit that provides a framework and certification for companies wishing to benefit society as well as their shareholders. There is a growing community of more than 1,600 certified B Corps from 42 countries and over 120 industries (many of which are SMEs). These companies have signed up to meet rigorous standards of social and environmental performance, accountability and transparency in order to redefine success in business (B Corporation.net, n.d.; B Corporation.uk, n.d.).

Reflection on your company's role in the community

What is the impact that your company is making on the immediate community and broader system?

Reflection on sustainability

Is sustainability a mere tick-box exercise in your company or is it part of the overall business strategy? What action could you take today to better balance short-term and long-term interests?

About the author

Palma Michel is a qualified lawyer, mindful leadership advisor, executive coach, meditation teacher and sought-after public speaker. She is the co-founder of Profuse29. Her clients include CEOs, creatives, philanthropists, high-potentials, global multinationals, SMEs and start-ups.

Palma previously spent ten years as a board-level executive search consultant (Principal-level) with two of the world's leading executive search firms Heidrick & Struggles and Korn/Ferry International in Europe, Asia and the UK. She has over a decade's worth of experience in advising and coaching top CEOs, boards and investors on senior leadership issues.

A sought-after public speaker, she regularly speaks about the link between mindfulness and creativity, mindful working, mindful leadership and mindful living and has been hosted by the London School of Economics, The Fiorucci Art Trust, Google Campus, Second Home, The Soho House Group and Jamie Oliver's Big Feastival.

To get in touch with Palma visit palmamichel.com

●Profuse29

Profuse29 is a holistic consultancy which offers science-driven courses in mindfulness to individuals and organisations.

By offering contemporary and science-driven meditation courses, Profuse29 aims to promote the benefits of contemplative practice within modern-day cosmopolitan society.

To find out more about our mindfulness programmes for leaders and teams visit profuse29.com

'As a start-up entrepreneur, Palma's guidance on mindfulness is the key to my own inner oasis, which is an eternal, peaceful ground that I can always return to during the many ups and downs in entrepreneurship.'

Ada Yi Zhao
Founder and CEO of Curated Crowd,
a part of Curated Ventures

'Palma was a godsend to us! She came to us for eight weeks and taught us how to shut out the noise, let go of negative and distracting thoughts and find the stillness where creativity flourishes.'

Caitlin Ryan
Executive Creative Director, Cheil UK

Bibliography

Ames, D., Brockner, J. and Benjamin, L. (2012) Listening and interpersonal influence. Available at: http://www8.gsb.columbia.edu/researcharchive/articles/4938 Accessed: 15/12/16.

Ayala, N. (2014) Q&A with Ellen Langer. J. Walter Thompson Intelligence. Available at: http://bit.ly/2lwAv8G Accessed: 15/01/17.

B Corporation.net. (n.d.) B Corporation. Available at: https://www.bcorporation.net/ Accessed: 15/12/16.

B Corporation.uk. (n.d.) B Corporation UK. Available at: http://bcorporation.uk/ Accessed: 15/12/16.

Bailey, S. (2015) 'The huge value of mindfulness at work: An interview with Ellen Langer'. *Forbes*. Available at: http://bit.ly/2kcLRxA Accessed: 15/12/16.

Begley, S. and Davidson, R. (2012) *The Emotional Life of Your Brain*. Hodder & Stoughton.

Brewer, J. (2016) *A simple way to break a bad habit*. Ted.com. Available at: http://bit.ly/1OUI0Uj Accessed: 15/12/16.

Bolte Taylor, J. (2008) *My Stroke of Insight: A brain scientist's personal journey*. Hodder & Stoughton.

Carnegie, D. (2008) *How to Win Friends and Influence People*. Prabhat Books.

Clegg, A. (2014) 'The quiet art of being a good listener'. *The Financial Times*. Available at: http://on.ft.com/2mealnb Accessed: 06/03/2017.

Congleton, C., Hölzel, B. and Lazar, S. (2015) 'Mindfulness can literally change your brain'. *Harvard Business Review*. Available at: http://bit.ly/1wy1AH1 Accessed: 15/12/16.

Duhigg, C. (2016) 'What Google learned from its quest to build the perfect team'. *The New York Times*. Available at: http://nyti.ms/2jNEz4Q Accessed: 15/12/16.

Drucker School of Management. (2016) Executive Mind Leadership Institute, Drucker School of Management. Available at: http://drucker.cgu.edu/affiliates/executive-mind-leadership-institute/ Accessed: 15/12/16.

euronews. (2015) 'Exploring the brain while we chat to better understand how it works'. Available at: www.euronews.com/2015/06/30/exploring-the-brain-while-we-chat-to-better-understand-how-it-works Accessed: 15/12/16.

Fox, J. (2012) 'Habits: Why we do what we do'. *Harvard Business Review*. Available at: https://hbr.org/2012/06/habits-why-we-do-what-we-do Accessed: 10/01/17.

Frankl, Victor E. (2006) *Man's Search for Meaning*. Beacon Press.

Fredrickson, B. (2003) 'The value of positive emotions'. *American Scientist*. Available at: http://www.americanscientist.org/issues/pub/the-value-of-positive-emotions/5 Accessed: 15/01/17.

Goleman, D. (2006) *Emotional Intelligence*. Bantam Books.

Goleman, D. (2014) *Focus: The hidden driver of excellence*. Bloomsbury.

Goleman, D. (2015a) *A Force for Good*. Bloomsbury.

Goleman, D. (2015b) *The Executive Edge: An insider's guide to outstanding leadership*. More Than Sound.

Gorlick, A. (2009) 'Media multitaskers pay mental price, Stanford study shows'. Available at: http://news.stanford.edu/2009/08/24/multitask-research-study-082409/. Accessed: 15/12/16.

Greater Good. (n.d.) 'For too long, we've taken gratitude for granted'. Available at: http://greatergood.berkeley.edu/expand inggratitude Accessed: 15/12/16.

Hanson, Rick (n.d.) 'Confronting the negativity bias'. Available at: http://www.rickhanson.net/how-your-brain-makes-you-easily-intimidated/ Accessed 15/01/17.

Harvard Business Review Staff. (2013) 'The multitasking paradox'. *Harvard Business Review*. Available at: https://hbr.org/2013/03/the-multitasking-paradox Accessed: 15/12/16.

INSEAD. (2007) 'Results of major research project on corporate social responsibility'. Available at: https://www.insead.edu/news/2007-response Accessed: 15/12/16.

Kanter, R.M. (2011) 'How great companies think differently'. *Harvard Business Review*. Available at: https://hbr.org/2011/11/how-great-companies-think-differently Accessed 15/12/16.

Kramer, G. (2012) *Insight Dialogue: The personal path to freedom*. Shambala.

Langer, E. (2014) *Mindfulness*. Da Capo Press.

Levitin, D. (2014) *The Organized Mind*. Penguin.

Levitin, D.J. (2015) 'Why the modern world is bad for your brain'. *The Guardian*. Available at: http://bit.ly/1UriXpS Accessed: 15/12/16.

Marano, H.E. (2003) 'Our brain's negative bias'. *Psychology Today*. Available at: https://www.psychologytoday.com/articles/200306/our-brains-negative-bias Accessed: 15/12/16.

Mindfulness All-Party Parliamentary Group (2015) Mindful Nation UK. Available at: www.themindfulnessinitiative.org.uk/images/reports/Mindfulness-APPG-Report_Mindful-Nation-UK_Oct2015.pdf Accessed: 10/01/17.

Reynolds, G. (2016) 'How meditation changes the brain and the body'. *The New York Times*. Available at: http://nyti.ms/2jHhyi6 Accessed: 24/02/17.

Seppala, E. (2015) 'How meditation benefits CEOs'. *Harvard Business Review*. Available at: https://hbr.org/2015/12/how-meditation-benefits-ceos Accessed: 15/12/16.

Spiegal, A. (2008) 'Hotel maids challenge the placebo effect'. NPR. Available at: www.npr.org/templates/story/story.php?storyId=17792517 Accessed: 10/01/17.

Tlalka, S. (2016) 'How science reveals that "well-being" is a skill'. Mindful. Available at: www.mindful.org/science-reveals -well-skill Accessed: 15/12/16.

Wikipedia. (n.d.) 'Meditation'. Available at: https://en.wikipedia .org/wiki/Meditation Accessed: 15/12/16.

Woollaston, V. (2015) 'How often do YOU check your phone? Average user picks up their device 85 times a DAY – twice as often as they realise'. *Daily Mail*. Available at: http://dailym .ai/1GPs1mm Accessed: 15/12/16.

Zeidan, F., Johnson, S., Diamond, B., David, Z. and Goolkasian, P. (2009) 'Mindfulness meditation improves cognition: Evidence of brief mental training'. Available at: www.gwern.net/docs /dnb/2010-zeidan.pdf Accessed: 15/12/16.

Notes

Notes

Your vision will become clear only when you can look into your own heart. Who looks outside, dreams; who looks inside, awakes.

Carl Jung

Other Authority Guides

The Authority Guide to
Practical Mindfulness:
How to improve your productivity,
creativity and focus by slowing down for
just 10 minutes a day

Tom Evans

Enhance your wellbeing, creativity and vitality with mindfulness meditation.

In this *Authority Guide*, Tom Evans, invites you to embrace the benefits of meditation in both your life and your business. With the practical mindfulness meditative techniques described in this book, you will learn how to get more done in less time. You will discover how to generate ideas off the top of your head and how to allow serendipity to land at your feet. This book opens the door to a new way to be and do.

The Authority Guide to Meaningful Success:
How to combine purpose, passion and promise to create profit for your business

Tim Johnson

Business results and meaningful work connect to impact effectiveness in our organisations and lives.

Tim Johnson, founder of Meaningful Success, shows you how to integrate practical business thinking with practical personal development to create global impact through your business or charity. This *Authority Guide* blueprints how we can embrace the best elements of entrepreneurial drive and passion, and an enabling blame-free culture to lead high-performing teams whilst providing personal fulfilment for all.

The Authority Guide to Emotional Resilience in Business: Strategies to manage stress and weather storms in the workplace

Robin Hills

How do your challenges inside and outside of work impact upon your emotions and your resilience?

The emotional resilience of those involved in a business will contribute significantly to the organisation's success. This *Authority Guide* from leading emotional intelligence expert, Robin Hills, will help you change the way you think about yourself and the way you approach potentially difficult situations. You will be able to develop your own personal resilience and understand how to develop resilience within the hearts and minds of your team and your organisation.

We hope that you've enjoyed reading this *Authority Guide*. Titles in this series are designed to offer highly practical and easily-accessible advice on a range of business, leadership and management issues.

We're always looking for new authors. If you're an expert in your field and are interested in working with us, we'd be delighted to hear from you. Please contact us at commissioning@suerichardson.co.uk and tell us about your idea for an *Authority Guide*.